D0911080

DUSK & DUST

DUSK&
DUST

ESTEBAN RODRÍGUEZ   POEMS

Emma Rose,
I hope you enjoy
and that you find
your voice.

HUB CITY PRESS
SPARTANBURG, SC

Copyright © 2019
Esteban Rodríguez

All rights reserved. No part of this book may be reproduced in any form
or by any electronic means, including information storage and retrieval systems,
without permission in writing from the publisher, except by a reviewer,
who may quote brief passages in a review.

Editor: Patrick Whitfill
Cover and book design: Kate McMullen
Cover image: Cindy Watson, www.flickr.com/photos/cindylouboo

Library of Congress Cataloging-in-Publication Data

Names: Rodríguez, Esteban, 1989- author.
Title: Dusk & dust / Esteban Rodriguez.
Other titles: Dusk and dust
Description: Spartanburg, SC : Hub City Press, 2019.
Identifiers: LCCN 2018060282 | ISBN 9781938235559
Classification: LCC PS3618.O35823 A6 2019
DDC 811/.6—dc23

LC record available at https://lccn.loc.gov/2018060282

Hub City Press gratefully acknowledges support from Amazon Literary Partnership
and the Chapman Cultural Center in Spartanburg, South Carolina.

HUB CITY PRESS
186 W. Main Street
Spartanburg, SC 29306
864.577.9349 | www.hubcity.org

for María Elena

CONTENTS

CHRISTMAS

I used to imagine snow quilted over rows of *colonia* rooftops, a blanket of white disguising poverty, erasing the patchy asphalt shingles shriveled like the skin of a spoiled tomato. I imagined my house wasn't stitched together with Home Depot wood, slabs of gray brick stacked and restacked to form another wall, a future bedroom for my baby sister, a frame that never obeyed my father's invented geometry. He was always building something, the same car engine, a crooked driveway he'd never finish, yearly promises for a better home, new neighbors, flower-patterned wallpaper, central heating so we wouldn't keep the stove top on when the weather got cold, those unfair winds seeping through towels nailed like crosses around our windows. Winters never dropped below 50 in the Valley, yet there we were: Father, Mother, Son hiding from the temperature beneath layers of sheets and pillows, flea market coats and sweaters, restless limbs pressed and bound to each other's warmth, hostage to a torn linoleum floor. I imagined waking up on Christmas morning, the Rockefeller tree in the center of our living room, neon lights softly strung, the scent of suburbia and pine needles perfuming my nostrils, eyes spellbound by the ornaments flickering glittery gold, and below: a horde of store-wrapped gifts placed around a shoebox filled with snow, my tiny hands digging for a childhood I'd want to remember, a blueprint for memories that would never melt.

LUCHA LIBRE

It was the mask I wanted more
than fame, the tight turquoise leather
tied with red shoestring around my nape,
the thought of being someone else
without being anchored to a face,
so as not to face the features in the face
that were slowly changing, growing
stranger by the year. And there was
the white complexion so different from
the darker shades of skin around me,
and the pimples unwilling to renounce
their loyalty, leaving me to reinvent
the candy-red bumps as chickenpox instead.
Even if I didn't know the one-hit wonder
of this disease, once I saw those Mexican
men fighting on TV, I couldn't care less
if anyone else believed it, if I, like them,
was putting up a front because a front
was the surest thing to guise myself in,
to carry my confidence further than
their choreographed jumps, than their lunges,
plunges, angelic dives, than the tiptoe
rope-walking as they back-flipped farther
into the ring, or as their sweaty bodies
began to sync with the crowd's shock
and awe, feed off their praise and screams.
And there I was, bouncing off my bed,
mumbling Spanish I could barely speak,
and hardly able to drop-kick, eye-poke,
cross chop, pile drive, head-butt, body slam,
brain-bust, somersault, shoulder claw,
slingshot or sleeper hold into my role

as *rudo*, the dirty-playing villain desperate
to pin the appearance I no longer wanted,
to wait for the count and finish off
with a headlock so I wouldn't have to take off
my mask, reveal to myself who I knew
I really was.

FENCE

We weren't exactly tourists anymore, amateurs at crossing over,
    tossing change
and lint inside their half-cut, empty jugs of milk, nodding as they
    blessed us

from behind the fence; their scabbed fingers anchored to the plastic's
    jagged edge,
heavy with the weight of pity, stares. We weren't exactly shocked by all
    the begging

at the border, the women sprawled outside the bridge, sleeping children
    cradled
in serapes, strapped like hammocks below their mother's breasts,
    as hordes of flies

dove at their eyelids and crawled across their swollen cheeks. As sad
    as the scene
was supposed to be, I still had fun feeding quarters down the slot,
    swinging past

the metal arms, the rattle from the turnstile louder than pennies dancing
    inside a can.
We'd matured from trivialities, group photos at the flagpole,
    at the emblem

of an eagle with a snake perched above a cactus, copper cruelly
    chipping off,
a metaphor for the landscape of this country. At ten, I had no
    metaphors

for barefooted boys selling Chiclets like insurance, running after
    every passerby,

tugging their sleeves, nagging how their gum was cheaper than
   the other guys'.

But *diez centavos* was too desperate to translate to my mother's ears,
   and even though
she spoke their language, she used her English silence to mute
   their pleas; those shouts

for discount pharmaceuticals, healing herbs and Freon, strings of garlic
   and streetside
taco stands drenched in spices I had never smelled. We were them
   without the burden

of being them, shared last names with them, an economic convenience
   living so close
to them, but when my mother tugged me closer to her waist, clenched
   the collar

of my white and sweaty shirt, I heard the tension in her grip saying
   I was not,
would never be one of them, would play the role of 'in-between' instead,
   the relative

from *el otro lado*, the boy straddled on the valley of two geographies,
   walking over
with his stoic, middle-aged mother, unaware that her stay-at-home salary
   didn't come

with dental, that her enamel was dissolving, riddled with cavities across
   her molars,
where she'd thrust and dig with toothpicks, nails, scoop out the half-
   chewed gunk

of food, repeat the rhythm after every meal. And there came a point
    when all she scraped
was nerve and gum, when her habit spread into years of sleeplessness,
    aggravated

by a dentist speaking Spanish too clinical to understand: drilling, talking,
    drilling,
pausing, yanking out the reasons why we made our trips, those weekend
    afternoons

crossing back high on anesthesia and lobby candy, staggering past
    the line of women
still staring through the heavy mesh, and still melting along the shadeless
    pavement,

wondering, I imagined, how our sloppy smiles tasted.

CACTUS

Mid-August. The last of July's clouds curdle
like expired milk, stain the dry Bermuda grass
with shifting Rorschach shadows, and with a sense
the afternoon will offer nothing more than sweat
and stale air. I sit and watch the parched cactus
perched along the splintered porch-rail: pot-ridden,
small, ripe with polka-dotted patches of green skin
peeling off, with a crown of spines cloaked
in a history of dirt, and worn by the sudden flares
of gravel rising locust-like around our home,
feeding every notion that the rain has fled,
become a fugitive spread like folklore in the north.
Not even God can save this place from geography,
not even the devil wants his fever back, an old spell
he cast, but couldn't force himself to love,
as the rare breeze I love scuttles across my father's
barren scalp, then moves down the bandana noosed
around his neck, the brown and sweat-clotting pores
of middle-age flesh, that entire arthritic skeleton
that resurrects into its daily chores again, relentless
like the sun, and that like the open grave of land
he was born on, has evolved to embrace the slow
embalming heat; the blisters, the burns, the small
stampede of mangy cattle he wrangles in our corral.
Though I feel the need to help him with another
day's work, I hold back when his body language
suggests my hands are too young and handsome,
when I see his thick and scabbed calluses mapped
on his palms, and feel my own gripping the soft pad
of a ballpoint pen, sketching the cactus and him
along my textbook margins, because even if
this afterschool image was fading before I started,

decomposing like papyrus, at least there's enough
space here for them to live, and for me to sketch
myself between them, let my stick-figure body
bleed through every page, wondering who,
if anyone, will find these portraits next year,
if they'll study the way our faces melted, visualize
what little life there was for us to absorb.

DOGS

Yowling, as if the space beneath our house bears a new one every night, they slither out, one by one against a pre-dawn haze of gnats and light, a pack of mutts with their younger mutts trailing close behind; the top of their muzzles ripe with mucus leaking from their eyes; their spines cloaked in ashen earth, and sprinkled bits of splintered oak gnawed by termites beneath the porch, that excavated den they've made their home. These are far from the Lassies trained for TV shows, the barnyard family pets, or workdogs guiding goats from the pasture in, but strays exhausting every place they've ever been, like nomads trudging through some bible desert, still without a place to go, aware that every inch of here is bruised with thirst, and that the ground brands their feet with scalded mounds of dirt. But I am just a boy, squatting low, crawling far beneath the steps, placing slabs of ham against the broken bricks, concerned their feral habits haven't fully formed, that they'll wander all day without a thing to eat, no bone or chow placed inside a bowl; that the mothers of the pack will return with teats still leather-black, wary that as I belly out this wooden womb, they'll have to worry about another mouth that isn't full.

TELENOVELA

I was born to a line of housewives obsessed with living more dramatically, devoted mothers immersed in Mexican telenovelas, those afternoon marathons built on the same basic plot: handsome Latin Boy falls for gorgeous Latin Girl, jealous ex-lovers scheme to break them apart. Their struggle aggravated by conniving aunts and uncles, pregnant maids and mistresses, rich and misleading step-fathers usurping everyone's camera time, eager to push their way into frame when the scene shifts to a shirtless farmhand, slowly pans across his young and hairless chest; those polished blots of sweat dilating my mother's eyes with subplots of haystack sex. To sit and watch her sit and watch another episode was an episode in and of itself: the rising action of her middle-aged and plus-sized body rising to adjust the foil-wrapped antenna, to smack the hiccup static from the box, catch the out-of-wedlock drama, it's sharp and sudden orchestra coupled with another *Julio, tu eres el papá!* Because every twist fed her confidence, she'd nudge me to lift my shoes off the couch, mimicking every multitasking mother who controlled the show, women she imagined herself to be, as I imagined her inner-monologue saying she wanted out, courage to break the spell of having a household to clean, of cooking for a husband whose sun-branded skin secreted wet cement, filled the kitchen with a scent she tried to kill with Pine-Sol and potpourri. I could see her taking mental notes on how to fake a death, on the latest ways to use mascara, comb her knotted hair, hold back the waterworks when Boy was losing Girl, or when again a *novela* was about to end. And she'd turn to me as if I were the boy cast solely for his smile, to provide some sort of cute and comic relief, or comments so innocently profound they'd linger beyond the screen, beyond the shadows of the kitchen table where she helped me master English with her broken English, reading story after story like lines off a script, and rehearsing every scene where the mother sighs, hugs her son, accepts the role she knows she has to play.

FAIR

And as March thaws the last of winter's
vagrant winds, dusk smears what's left of itself
across the fair's parking lot, that shadowed grid
of cars and trucks where I watch the Ferris wheel
spin against a pink and purple sky, seep over
the silhouettes of mini-roller coasters, tattered tents,
a rusted stadium where the crowd cheers for one
fallen cowboy after the next. Regardless of the season,
no amount of change can erase the scent of cattle shit,
or the prized array of fragrances that linger near
the ticket booths, where I fall in line, accept
this smell everyone ahead of me accepts; a trade-off
for a chance at fun, or what fun can be had
from ping pong balls, fishbowls, dull darts,
balloons, rubber duck ponds, water guns, rope ladders,
or the *Ring the Bell* crowded with boys eager
to swing its chained mallet through the air.
As I walk past them—note their willingness
to be quantified by the height their light reaches—
the carnies, with their greased and tobacco-stained
faces, holler for my attention, as if they can sense
the same need for overcompensation; their voices
shrieking with the promise of rewards. And yet,
because another year has passed since impulse
led me in their direction, I settle for the consolation
of knowing that even the simplest things are rigged,
that as the bright myriad of games dilate into a panorama,
and the evening spreads like a pinned moth across
the lot, I must push my way deeper through the fair,
until, like a segue meant to expose the villain
within ourselves, I find myself inside a house
of mirrors, a puzzle of convex and concave curves

distorting me into shapes I've never felt, into anatomies
rearranged with anorexia, elephantiasis, or reflections
of my endless face as it slowly melts, swells
into whatever figure the glass wants me to be,
or that I'll continue projecting onto myself
even when I emerge from its illusion,
and rechristen my senses to the funnel cake
and cotton candy air, to the polka-steps
and accordions, and to the deep-fried moon
tucked away like a secret sideshow—its glow
leaving me with the night's only souvenir.

PIÑATA

Still, the tangled mesh and papier-mâché held,
and as it hung from the branch with the chosenness
of a sacrificial lamb, its body bled a stream
of lollipops and mini-chocolate bars on the parched
Bermuda grass, where cousins I had never met
kneeled like tired field workers, bundling
their cravings inside shirttails and hands.
As much as I wanted to scoop my own stash,
as hard as I swung, side-stepped the wrecking ball
of fun till the itchy crown of sweat completed
its exodus to my jaw, I kept staring up, awed
at the battered lumps, at the news-printed intestines
held by glue and starch, and at the angle in which
the piñata dangled beneath the afternoon gallows
of shade and sun, where my father, like a puppeteer
merely feigning his clumsiness, orchestrated
its chaos farther up, and flung it toward my face
even as I struck the burro's neck and back;
how the rainbow-colored hooves flew like shrapnel
across the lawn, constellating near the crowd
of relatives chanting for the blows I landed,
applauding the swipes that ached my arms
into a sense that I should stop, put the broomstick
down, and touch its mangled limbs with a feeling
I could almost claim as guilt.

SALT

My grandmother picks one from the basket, not yet moldy, but already pockmarked, tender, its skin molded to her grip. She slices the tomato down the middle, calm, slowly; the seedy juice gushing along the counter, the salt spread from the shaker with her fingertips, each granule pressed deeper, as if trying to heal the wound she just created. I am midway through my lunch, and she is starting on her snack, dessert, whatever she calls this habit of scraping tomato against her gums, sucking out all the salt, then pouring more, as I know she isn't really hungry, but attempting to revive her dead nerve endings; the black and jagged teeth spread like a broken window inside her mouth, where I imagine her speech gets caught, where the words try to crawl out like children escaping an abandoned house, this vitiligo flesh of her aging body. Even if she's forgotten how conversations once tasted, the way she used to call my name in Spanish when I could not yet understand it, she hands me the unsalted half, leans over, slides the shaker on the table; the kitchen knife gripped in her other hand, as she stands waiting to see if I'll put salt, if I can chew the silence her tongue can no longer savor.

WHITE GOLD

Soon after, I'd weave through the rows of severed stalk,
through the fallow soil where dusk would chalice into a panorama,

and where the horizon, unacquainted with any climate beyond
its own drought, would embrace the distant scythes of lightning

too faint to coax the local crows into migrating, too sterile to muffle
the wind's warm and heavy pouting. On nights when the moon

hovered just below the womb of constellations, and the sleepwalking
breeze filtered through the curtains, I'd watch the neighboring fields

of sugarcane retire from the heat; how those swollen harvests sighed
for hours with relief, extending their personification to the morning,

when again dawn, like a wound reopened, secreted between
the waning folds of darkness, while the slight chill, squatting

like a fugitive, retreated from the air's humid custody. But even
suffering has an expiration date, and as the sun dilated across

the plains, bleaching the afternoon beyond its inherent coloring,
the unmarked water trucks would arrive, soak the perimeter down,

while off to the side, my father and a handful of men did their best
impression of God and watched this coordinated baptism unfold

with folded arms, waiting for the cane to dry enough before combing
the field with propane torches, before molding the fire I'd learn

to shape as part of my inheritance, and letting their flames canopy
the stalk; the scene mimicking the napalmed jungles of Vietnam,

or whatever event history could lend where a crowd gathered
and gawked as the blaze quickly spread, unwilling to stop.

And yet, despite my attempt to give history a role, my father kept it
a private affair, a ritual he and his men would tread back from,

inhaling the sharp scent of sucrose, and skirting the plumes of smoke
as we stood surveying the ashen ceremony of carbon, the cane's

crackling chorus, the raw and boiled juice ready for extraction.

VENTRILOQUIST

No spotlight, no stage or stagecraft,
no props or voices prompting laughter
from an audience, no hand but the hand
I use to lift this dummy from a box
casted to the back of my parents' closet.
Because backstories are hard to connect
with, I make no attempt to uncover
the reasons it's been forgotten, assume
it's a collectable, a gag gift, a memento
dressed in the same black and baggy suits
all grandfathers are buried in. I press
his shoulder to my chest, run my palm
through his blond and poorly stitched hair,
over his cheeks coated with blush,
that coquettish constellation of freckles,
that cold skin that feels as though
an embalmer had given it its final touch.
Though slack-jawed and broken,
his mouth is still sculpted for monologues
and conversations, for the right moment
to slip in another punch-line, to continue
wherever his performance left off; tell a joke,
sing a song, practice switching between
two lexicons until a middle ground is found,
the way I—a son descended from diasporas—
spoon-feed myself a second alphabet
I can't pronounce, unable to distinguish
between accents, when and where to use
the single and double *r*'s, or to dislodge
the diphthongs clumped like excess saliva
around my gums, inflecting my diction
into a dialect of doubt, and going so far

as to abbreviate the emphasis of certain
vowels. I listen to the *E* in my first name
slip from the *s* it's been paired with,
while my lips, chapped with the English
I love, slowly repeat a catalogue of code-
switching adjectives and nouns, phrases
and idioms, kitchen table lectures my father
always begins with a *Que chingaos*,
or the Spanish my mother uses to indicate
the severity of a subject, *Esteban,*
tu papá te está esperando en el corral.
And there are tildes, inflections, gender-
specific pronouns I mismatch and write down
on a Babel of post-its, intending to later
figure out, remembering that suitcase
of grammar my parents' parents carried
over, and which remained untranslated
when it reached its second generation,
settled on my tongue, because like this dummy
relying on the voices around him for reference,
I'll replicate whatever speech I'm taught,
feeling that regardless of the worlds
I live in, I'll be mouthing a language
that was never mine to inherit.

L I P S

Despite his implanted plastic devil horns, his filed
front teeth, the spiked collar and the white cartoon-sized
bowtie hanging at his chest like a rosary, his shrunken
top hat, the metal piercings protruding like half-hammered
nails across his cheeks, his earlobes melting past his jawline,
and the full-body tattoos arranged into labyrinths of black
and neon ink—each straining to bleed beyond the surface,
to become its own backstory in bas-relief—what awed me most
was the man's sagging bottom lip, the way it dangled
like a noose threaded loosely out of meat, swinging back
and forth when he bowed, took off his vest, and as if stretching
a tire to fit a rim, began squeezing in a gauge as thick
as a paint can's lid, as inch by inch, he extended his flesh
further into its self-inflicted exaggeration. That summer,
August forgot to hand its climate to fall, bleached the days
together like a ghost town billboard, and while the flies
advertised our skin as future carcasses, and dusk
kept my father and I wondering if its bruise would ever end,
we did our best impressions of a father and son roaming
the lesser known parts of the circus: the tents filled
with deformities and fortune tellers, the tables lined
with jars of eyes, brains and testicles, or that contraption
hoisting a woman by her shoulder blades and shadow,
where she hovered like a broken wind chime, and jostled
with the confidence that modification was indeed an art form,
or was at least appealing enough to draw a crowd in, to employ
the bearded milk-chugging baroness, the androgynous three-
legged crawler, and the corseted Siamese sword-swallowers,
who in their mannequin-like demeanor, performed their acts
with the same etiquette as the man still locking the gauge
inside his lips, and still standing earnestly to the half-
opened eyes around him, to the way I too couldn't help
but want my body sculpted past its ordinariness.

MOSQUITOES

Though slow to accept the burden
of another morning, the sun, like an old bulb
flickering back into its wattage, pools
along the tilled horizon, polishes
the front yard with enough perspective
to believe the patches of parched grass
are begging for a more suburban description,
for the harmony of scheduled sprinklers,
trimmed and even edges, for a fence
to embody the distinction between *ours*
and *theirs*, or anything beyond the quilted
moisture teasing the air's expectation
for rain, and softening enough soil to harbor
hordes of newborn mosquitoes ready
to fever this fevered stretch of ground,
to campaign their blood politics on the closest
body their proboscis can claim, and spread
hypotheticals of dengue, West Nile, new strains
of malaria, and bouts of night sweats that blot
our bedridden skin like dew. Even in flight,
their chaos lacks a cure, and as they dart, dive,
and hover into view, I can't help but admire
their dance from eradication, the beauty
in surviving and finding a way to thrive
in the right tropic-like temperature all year,
and in not knowing that they'll only live
to the end of the week, that when I walk
through their ritual, and my sweat
becomes sweet, they'll swarm around me
with their messy tango, surprised
when my hands begin to take the lead.

TOOTHLESS

After lunch, I'd stare as my grandfather pulled them from his mouth, spellbound by the splash, by the way they sunk the only way dentures sink: steady, slow, soaked in a glass half-filled with water, in a pocket of bubbles rising to the wavy horizon before the saliva wobbled to the bottom. It was as if the plastic resin still held his breath, a sigh, a curse, another crude and muffled comment about my grandmother's cooking, how her soggy saltless rice stuck to his roof like glue; his tongue too thick and jaundiced to dig out the food. Unlike him, I was adjusting to my second set, to the incisors sprouting like a crooked, white-picket fence, and to every silver crown that had yet to loosen from the root. Everything I ate had a hint of metal, blood or chicken, and even if I couldn't taste the difference, I slouched with my grandfather on the sofa, pretended to share his disapproval, pretended my buds were victims to a healthy diet, as I tried to imagine the slush of tobacco that once chewed through his enamel, because despite how naïve and neglectful I was of my own brushing habits, I envied the ease with which he could abandon language, throw speech in a glass to lounge on the table. I wanted his slack-jawed drool, the nap through the afternoon news, the groan and gruff when he'd wake up, squeeze his cheeks and lock his teeth in place. And when his cravings ached, when my grandmother's anti-sugar crusade held no weight, he snuck me out to town, and with the arthritis that defined his strength, lifted my body above the counter, where a parade of flavors smiled behind the frosty window, and where our lips, chapped with the side effects of neglect, quivered till we rewarded them with sweetness.

MEAT

As I run my hand along the long display case
stacked with columned slabs of meat,
my cold reflection blurs between every nose-,
cheek- and palm-printed smudge, and warps
across the sharp and uncleaned scree of ice,
where half-packed and scattered like rusted
pawn-shop jewelry—like yard sale items
a day's worth of eyes have yet to want—
lie pork chops, sausage-links, bacon strips
and mounds of bone-in and boneless beef,
as well as chicken breasts, legs and feet,
and ambiguous, primal cuts draped in a quilt
of seasoned salt. Even with the small and split
carcasses hanging in the back, or the bags
of charcoal pressed against my knees,
the market's staleness stems mainly from
the butcher himself, that sweaty, middle-aged
and mustached man who's *How much?*
spills across the counter like a contradiction,
because as low and disinterested as it sounds,
as detached from the art it appears it once was,
it's still a voice my father and I know to trust,
still focused on weighing the right amount,
and wrapping the few pounds we take home,
where we watch my nightgowned mother cook
each piece till they mirror the coarseness
of coffee grounds, and where with each bite,
I'm reminded that like the acres of grazing cattle
we passed on the drive back from town,
my own body is nothing more than meat,
than a sweaty figure slipping into the bedroom
after dinner, lying next to an overworking fan,

whose blades can't keep my cheeks from pooling
down my jaw, or from letting the night—seeping
through the window mesh—fever my flesh
until I'm no longer tender, raw.

HEIFER

Lethargically, and on the last leg of its orbit, the morning moon hangs above a heifer garroted on a knotted barbed-wire fence. She stabs a squeal into the air, lunges back and forth expecting to untangle her legs and neck, to unhook the rusted teeth clawing deeper into her flesh, as I claw my fingers through her sticky hair, pull her horseshoe-curved spine to my chest. She's trembling as if this were winter, as if she were old enough to know a climate that wasn't summer, and as her panting dampens my face, I imagine snow swirling above our heads, sprawled across the orphaned plains, falling at a pace that seems to soften the blood seeping from her ribs, that makes me believe I can find a hint of innocence in this event; that perhaps she won't remember the severity of her wounds, and I'll tread back home lending my father a quiet hand, forgetting how the wire's webbed around her skin like fate, how the force of every kick slowly wanes, and how I carve a stigmata through my palms and wrists, aware God is nowhere near this horizontal crucifixion, that the sacrifice isn't meant to be prophetic, but practical, a chance to resurrect her growing silence into a silence of afternoon grazing, so she can linger the way cattle have perfected the act of lingering, and I can watch from a distance, convinced even the bruised sky will heal itself.

TRASH

As bright as midnight underpasses lit with homeless fires,
or flares of summer fireworks singeing their signatures

across the air, the match swells, and my father bends the arthritic
architecture of his body down, squats with a can of diesel

in his hand, and douses a mound of trash he's piled
on the remnants of last month's ash. The moon, like a chipped

fingernail scratching the darkness, quickly arcs across the sky,
and as it casts a dim spotlight on the edge of our backyard,

every pair of nocturnal eyes eavesdrop on my father's stance,
on the way he tosses splintered crates and planks, scraps

of corrugated steel peeled from our unused shed, and car parts
weathered beyond repair. Like a magician pulling handkerchiefs

from a hat, he exhumes a stash of Hefty bags filled with cut brush
and grass, saw dust and roof shingles, a punctured water hose,

torn screen door mesh, along with a drawerful of my mother's
kitchenware, and aware that I'm always near, that I too

am an accomplice to this ritual, he pulls out a box of limbless
action figures too stiff and injured to play with again, too symbolic

for me not to notice, accept. I imagine, before the burning
begins, that he's building another house, framing a foundation

large enough for all the things this one can't fit, blueprinted
with a patio, a fence, a fertile lawn without the bent and rusted

hubcaps I sit on, or the stripped tires he lays on the heap
like funeral bouquets, stepping back as the blaze consumes

the mountain of our invented home, and as I amble toward it,
convinced that as the flames flare higher, we'll feel the need

to throw our tired bodies into the pyre.

INTERMISSION

June, like a fugitive outrunning spring's custody, squats across
the frontage road's vacant lot, where traveling trucks and trailers

pitch their portables and tents, plant rusted searchlights, and stake
faded signs for their weekend circus; an exhibition, which like a dream

meant to tie up loose ends, I find myself in again, caught in medias res,
but with the lucidity to sneak out before the next act begins,

wander off toward the half-lit outskirts of biblically rendered brush,
where poorly painted clowns blow their manifestos of Marlboro,

chit-chat and lunge phlegm-riddled bits of lipstick across the patchy,
sandpaper grass. These aren't the hungry demons feeding off

urban-legend flesh, or the on-screen fools who jump, smack,
and piggyback until cartoon stars sprout brightly from their heads,

but hired men dressed in mismatched sets of greasy clothes, oversized
shoes, cotton-candy wigs, personas they practice on until they perfect

every gimmick of their scripts, and their scripts become a part of them,
embodiments of how the self is lost behind real and imagined curtains,

of how there is no world beyond the migrant map of their skin,
or the notion that even when they're off the clock, far from their mini-

tricycles and coliseums, they're still inventing new tricks, twisting
balloons into poodles, giraffes, or juggling chainsaws and pins

with a sense that life doesn't always guarantee an intermission.
And as they stamp out their cigarettes, crouch back inside the tent,

I know I won't need to pay attention to the netless tightrope walkers,
to the fire-breathing sword swallowers, to the thick scent of elephant shit,

or to the glittery ringmaster, who, like a streetside prophet, shouts
that we should all be prepared, now that I've unveiled the performance

behind their performance, the age-old art of *The Show Must Go On*,
this newfound privilege that when the clowns taunt the focused tiger-tamers,

stop and bow, I'm the only one amongst the crowd with the right
to applaud like a shill.

SEASONAL

For a moment, they stand like retired scarecrows,
parched decoys for the fabled birds that never came.
Their distant silhouettes, gauzed by the morning fog,
dilate above my windowsill, shaping into middle-aged
bodies defined by every field they've ever migrated to,
by the rows of ambiguous crops they scoop between
their arms, and by the boxes they hold as they fill them
to the top, stack their quotas like cinder blocks
on the back of pickup trucks, and return to the harvest
still occupied with a homeless drought. Like a traveling
circus, they arrived unannounced, planted their portables
and tarps across the ground, and because the sky,
swollen with a stillborn climate, only bears a string
of malnourished clouds, the seasonal hands pick
what isn't already fated to rot. I watch how quickly
their foosball-figured bodies move back and forth,
how they keep their spines in a perfect arc,
while their sun-branded faces, stoic beyond
the need for explanation, mirror the rootless scabs
of dirt, and like the charred and crosshatched acres
of untilled earth, they endure heat not even God
or prayers to God have learned to cure, and perhaps
never will so long as the newborn flares of mirages
sprout, bleach the horizon from any sense of certainty,
and glaze every nameless worker with a terra cotta
skin, with the same fever further ossifying
the fossilized soil, yielding an indifference
no amount of sweat can sow itself into.

FOWL

No killing cone for this one, no quick and numb routine hoisting its body upside down, claws scratching the air, wings tunneled inside the flashing; a feather-full of impulse, struggle, and my father's knife sawing off its neck, bleeding like chickens do when it's time to bleed out. No, this one's mine, my Elena, this one he picks up, cradles in his arms, in the sweaty sleeves still fresh with after-scents of hay, manure. I couldn't hear what she heard from where I was standing, the humid afternoon spread across our backyard; his head titled, lips kissing the wet ruffle I kissed before he came out, before the screen slammed shut, and my mother's shouts echoed to a stop. But there was nothing he could say I couldn't see in his hands: louse feeding on her belly, pores unplucked, punch-red scars quilted with scabs as rough as tar; her pecks so sharp and accidental. Perhaps it was accident that brought us both together, that brought my father past the point of feeling sorry for his dilemma, twisting Elena's neck as if he were twisting mine, slow, severely delicate, looking away as he squeezed and snapped, waited for her clucks to go limp; the sun smeared along the wavy horizon, trembling like a spasm.

CLOTHESLINE

Like a congregation in mid-prayer, the Sunday morning winds
hum throughout the seared pews of dirt. Acres of cattle shit

and sagebrush preach their scent around the clothesline, settle
beneath the backdoor steps where I stand, gazing at the way

my disembodied father hangs, at how a row of wooden pins hoist him
by his soggy waist, and at the way in which patches of cement

ossify to his knees and thighs; the bleached and crosshatched denim
leaking at the pace of a broken faucet. Even as my shadow is branded

on the ground, that pair of Levi's thaws beside the brown and wrinkled
work shirts that define him at the ground he's paid to break; the thread

saturated into a résumé of sweat too thick to revise, erase. Back and forth,
he sways on the flaccid lines, thrusts his arms inside my mother's white

and parachuted blouses. The tipsy breeze flaps him closer, closer,
unbuttons her wardrobe further, but pulls him away when I walk over

and watch my mother, dressed in her weekend nightgown, fasten
our limbs to the lines, making us resemble forgotten Christmas lights,

or a set of Polaroids overexposed by the sun; the heat embalming
our catalogue of underwear, padded bras and mismatched socks,

the piss-blotted bed sheet I tuck myself in, assuming that memory,
like cotton, is thin enough to dry itself again, to remove the weight

it wasn't meant to hold, and to forget, when I'm pulled away,
the scent of soap puckered on my mother's hands, that attempt to scrub

our clothes until there were no stains left, until she believed,
since belief is all she has, that this was the week we'd start fresh.

LEMONADE

September sheds a calendar of unemployed leaves
along the plain's open palm, scatters their dead music
across the crosshatched lumps of ground, where the fingernails
of dawn crawl through the morning yawn of dew, scratch
and grip my grandmother's thirsty ankles, the worn-out soles
from her brown, diabetic shoes. Her nightgown-knees sink
along the border of the lemon tree's shadow, her small shadow
spills deeper in, where she separates a web of tangled, low-hanging
branches, severs the least shriveled lemons, and loads them
in a bowl before the sun's afternoon autopsy begins,
before another day passes, and the backyard armies of insects
carve colonies inside their acid skin. From the kitchen table
where I sit, near the torn and heat-warped window mesh,
I watch her stout and crooked vertebrae jut through the faded,
flower-patterned threads, uncoil carefully from its arched
position, from that steep and sharp angle at which her spine
used to hunch over Midwestern fields, sorting through
acresful of small, ambiguous crops, while at a few cents
an hour, still young and fast enough to resist the urge
of standing up, she'd stack another large basket, bucket
or box, and zigzag through a patchwork of farms
with another harvest to pluck, filling her daily quota
back to the top. Still, even muscle memory forgets
its intended purpose, and like rows of fallen and forgotten
citrus bulging through their sunburned skin, she slowly grew
out of her migrant flesh, shedding it between the castrated pores
of soil and the housing barracks she emptied out at the end
of every summer, aware that somewhere down the road,
she'd find herself bent at the feet of someone else, even if
it was just herself kneeling to the older woman she became,
to the way she staggers like a broken grocery cart back in,
tipping the bowl from her Rorschach-shaped hips, and flooding

the table with the future lemonade she's picked; a green
and pock-marked tide that never seems to end. And despite
her shrinking stature, the fact that her back has retired
into a stay-at-home posture, the subtle movements
in her body language haven't lost a step, haven't stopped
the lines on her forehead from gesturing that I squeeze
the pulp with my hands, drain the thin, sour blood
her jaundiced-colored tongue no longer has the patience
to lick; her palate too old and comatose to fix, and her wrists
too weak to move the bag of sugar I slide over, closer
to the pitcher, where like a child unfamiliar with packaged
plastic, she tears it open, and pours not a pinch, not a spoon,
not a cup, but enough to resemble the untouched sands
of a mapless island; a gulp of what I imagine
she once imagined as paradise, and which she now
tries to savor, smacking for flavor until her saliva
dries like paste around the chapped ruins of her lips.

LOCKS

Like the fading adhesive of an overused
stamp, the afternoon heat distances itself
from summer, from the months of humidity
the downtown trees have slowly matured from,
changing their leaves into shriveled shades
of orange, brown. Foliage scatters between
parking meters, lampposts, double-parked cars,
beneath the barbershop window's faint,
fluorescent sign, where debris flares up
at the pair of poles weathered of their stripes.
Inside, I scan the line of seated faces
too old with conversation to return a stare,
too retired on the daily craft of speech to shift
their focus, lift or readjust themselves, crank
their wrinkled necks from the sculpted sea
of foam; their lathered lives centered
on an oval frame of mirrors.

Not even the younger, hunched-over barbers
look up, shout more than a *Come in*
as my father explains they've already signed me in
on their mental list of who's next; their language
of regulars extended to us, reinforced with an echo
of trust, then phased out with the swift and shifting
melody of shears, the mechanical chorus of clippers
plowing through layered snowflakes of hair;
a small Christmas planted on each of their scalps,
sprinkled like polka dots around my father's ears,
and parted with a combed sense of sophistication
still decades from rooting on my head. I run
my fingers over the back of my neck, feel
almost ashamed my hair's the longest
and least aged in this room.

But even if the stack of magazines tear
like papyrus, and the slow and ancient beat
of what I think is jazz seeps through the plastic
stereo, the ceiling fan air mimics the same sense
of localness back home, the notion that the world
can be reduced to the smallest space and the most
uncomplicated people, to the bald-headed barber
who waves me over, adjusts and lowers his rusted,
red swivel throne.

And as my father stands behind us, mutters
small-talk and directions I can't make out,
I imagine my locks as wet ash falling to the ground,
as a shrapnel of strands smudged like black blood
around my temples and mouth, all of which
the barber cleans before he shapes a palmful
of cream around my jaw, aware there's nothing here
but empty follicles to shave off, and yet shaving
at the steady pace of his technique, as if pressing
the cold blade against my neck, my unpronounced
cheeks, is enough to make me acknowledge who I am,
or who I'll be when he takes the blue cape off,
because like a moth shedding the cocoon
from its wings, I'm given the space to shake
what my body doesn't need; my crosshatched
patches of rite sprawled along my feet,
swept up with pieces of a boy I know
I can no longer keep.

A X

Even after all the scrubbing, after every evening spent bowing to my reflection at the bathroom sink, I could smell the scent of dead bark on my hands, could feel the long handle of a crooked ax, the memory of its warm and splintered skin when I'd grip the belly tighter, hew log after log after log. There were no gloves or goggles, no time to think about how friction would reshape my fingerprints, or how easily wood split from wood if I never questioned my quota, if I believed that monotony would manifest into catharsis, or if I focused long enough to distract myself from what I was actually doing, set my silence on completing the backyard chores my father put me to work on every weekend. He told me we all needed to learn 'the lesson': discipline before duty, duty before knowing what it meant to work in this world for a living, and I sometimes thought this was either a dream or hallucination since he never spoke in metaphors, never lectured beyond simple body language, a nod or grunt when he handed me the ax, and I went to work striking the corroded blade through a thick ancestry of rings, through hours of the hickory haft burning into my already deciduous palms, while my imagination, feeding on the backcountry heat, made me a firefighter, a lumberjack, a sculptor who chiseled the wood into a different meaning, or a son who had every reason to construct a cabin inside his head, chop and store the old calendars of afternoons inside of it, and toss the warm catalogue of logs into a pile like bones, because even if my father saw this work as rite, as a seesaw of balance he envisioned I'd find, I could only envision myself naked on the porch, stripped of purpose and ready to harvest my blisters deeper inside these woods.

CATS

Belly blacker than asphalt, than fresh tire marks and the silhouettes of mesquite stenciled against a filmstrip sky, I squat to pay tribute, still an amateur in animal deaths, in stray cats I feed dinner-scraps against my mother's will. These are the driveway scavengers exhausted with garbage bins, solicitors of sympathy rubbing against my evening legs, and this is the dead one that veered off its map, tested traffic, briefly became brave. I study the lump of feral bone and flesh, how the miscellany of its stomach spreads like scree: rotten, red, scented with a sense that if I believe in fate, this is the only end it could have endured; that my presence is a kind of funeral, and the silence smeared like shit across my face is an elegy for all the lives this stretch of road has claimed, or for the feeling that I should toss it in the yard, dig a proper burial, and work through dusk even as the suburban moon—rising into our backcountry air—becomes a witness to the appendix of death again, to the way I scrape my shovel beneath the cat instead, dump it in a nearby bush, and turn back home with the hum of 281 singing in my ears.

S K I N

As if the mounted moose and raccoon heads weren't enough to induce
    queasiness,
I'd sit and listen to him explain his latest project in the basement,
    another black bear,

dabbling duck, some Doberman Pinscher a man couldn't part from
    his memory, heart.
The story's quite romantic till the skinning starts, the ease with which
    their frozen bodies

slide across the table; coolly steaming, slowly thawing, posed in the last
    moment
before the appendix of their deaths. If there was a god, he was
    a taxidermist

like my uncle, though less bearded and with more finesse at sculpting
    the still-life
of our bodies, more concern for the outer than our inner-workings.
    But God was nowhere

near the mannequins those weekend afternoons, the cold flesh wrapped
    around wood wool,
the slow stitching of their flaccid bellies, necks, or the placement
    of one glass eye

after another. Even then, I wanted to perform an autopsy on language,
    find a description
of how I felt when he tanned that white-tailed jackrabbit, not a job
    he got often,

but he'd often explain the legend of the jackalope, its hybrid antlers,
    hillside speed,

his handful of sightings on hunting trips. He told me that he sometimes
    put a flask

of Maker's Mark on the porch at night, found it empty in the morning,
    paw prints across
the front yard; that the jackalope's feral shyness resembled mine,
    and although I didn't see

the connection between me and something imaginary, I was convinced
    he was convinced
by its mythology, lured not by any desire to capture it, just retell
    the story. Perhaps

there's a gene that unthreads the sanity of all uncles, pushes them
    to the deep end
of the family pool, although he wasn't crazy as much as lonely, having
    hijacked my aunt's

patience with his hobby, drizzling details of his work into every
    conversation; touching
her cheeks with the after-scent of brine, and meat soaked in pickle acid
    and quilted salt.

Once, as I helped give form to a deer's flat head, he told me how he'd
    plan to stuff her
if he could, carve out her eyes, throw them on a plate, start cutting
    at the nape, down

the vertebrae, until he reached the border of her waist, and peeled
    her flesh like someone
peeling off a full-body swimsuit. When I asked about the organs,
    muscles, where he'd put

the skull, he said he'd bury them with her always wilted daffodils,
    her white garden cap,
and with the grass-etched gloves and handheld hoe she loved more
    than him. I tried

to laugh it off, but I knew he spoke seriously about his art, the potential
    to preserve his talent
through his wife, and, as he straightened out the snout, I remembered
    my aunt on the porch

one night, pale nightgown draped on the silent steps, her daffodil body
    stiff like a wolf's
drawn to the pine-needled moon, half-awake and drinking my uncle's
    whiskey.

EXODUS

Even if decades of laying cement have abbreviated his balance
and step, and his spine can no longer commit to symmetry—

curving like a question mark—my father continues to brush aside
his posture's battle with gravity, his joints' petition for retirement;

the concept having yet to migrate into meaning in either his broken
English or Spanish. Because routine is the only thing that keeps

his name on a payroll, he hauls his morning shadow into our kitchen's
Pine Sol-scented darkness, rubs away the few hours of sleep still loyal

to his eyelids, and bends at the counter like someone deep in prayer,
in the belief that he'll receive a better outcome if he remains longer

in his position. On mornings when he shuffles loudly through
   the drawers,
I eavesdrop from the hallway, watch him put his faith in the stained altar

of a coffee pot, in the stale fragrance of generic coffee grounds,
and in the wafer-thin filter where he pours them; the first spurt

popping like a muffled gun shot, then pooling into a puddle as thick
as the river he was reborn from. I listen to the ripples spread, fill

with the urgency of an hourglass, and I can't help but place him back
in the river again, dog-paddling to the other side, while the men
   squatting

to his rear, hoping the moonlight is qualified to be their ferryman,
test the water until they're wrapped inside its current, swimming

toward the lives they've already tilled on that fabled ground.
Slowly, my father reaches the muddy bank, bellies into the last leg

of his exodus, then into a husband defined more by his steel toes
    and hardhat,
or by the way in which he never has to cool the tumbler from its steam,

quickly sipping what he can before the sun, that ancient immigrant,
pierces the plains and clocks in, and before I walk in to finish whatever's

left, to taste that caffeinated oasis I can never sweeten enough to drink.

TAMALES

Late December, and the backyard trees shed
their leaves all afternoon, crease and toss their shadows
along the maze of exposed roots, while the canopies
of cross-hatched branches, stripped of their commitment
to make shade, become deciduous skeletons aligned
like figurines across the window frame, where despite
the appearance of winter, or the bruised body bag
of nightfall slowly covering the plains, the last
of autumn's lingering grip still leeches to the air,
seeps through the glass as I feel the humid breeze
graze my cheeks, noose my neck, until behind me,
where my mother and a handful of aunts gather,
the kitchen's slow-boiling smoke pulls me away.
The walls plume with the scent of chicken stock,
garlic, flour, sliced pork and onions, chili peppers
and overgenerous showers of salt, as well as platefuls
of cornhusks stacked into miniature towers, Babel-like
in their contorted structure, and pronounceable
only in a woman's palm. Though my mother and aunts
pass the stuffed tamales around, bend their housewife
backs like the teenage field workers they once were,
their round and middle-aged figures sway without
their usual definitions of work, and as they loosen
themselves from the posture they hold when there's
a public to hold it for—and I wonder why my uncles
and father aren't here to lend their callused hands—
the uneven linoleum cracks like arthritic bone
beneath my feet, and my aunts turn and stare at me,
as if I just broke a ritual I was never meant to know,
a rhythm they inherited of cooking tamales, garnishing
the night with laughter and forgetting it with tequila saved
from last year, because unlike the food they're tightly

wrapping, they unwrap themselves from who they are,
and embrace the new nakedness they could never
embrace alone, as their speech becomes tender, gummy,
and my mother, gauzed by the light, ambles over
to touch me, to feel the clenched and melting border
of my jaw, the hunger to understand what they know
is still too raw to eat.

LAST CALL

After my father would thrust his head in,
let his temples' cattle-scented sweat puddle
between the empty stacks of ice trays,
let the patchy savannah of his scalp imagine
a snowstorm in December, a black blizzard
barricaded in the back of our freezer, my mother,
hunched and braless in a nightgown,
would loudly stuff a pack of wine coolers in,
make it known that she was carving out
her time to relax, that as soon as the glass
and gold aluminum foil cooled to the point
that it burned her hands, she'd begin her dance
to the kitchen table, spread the bottles out
like a line of pawns, and one by one, erase
the evening heat that weighed her body down,
the thirst she knew would return
as a stronger thirst the next morning.

Unlike my father though, who dressed
his discretion in a paper bag or koozie,
she'd ebb between the low and loud of a weekend
bar, would one moment embody the tucked away
table still flirting with their pints of silence,
and the next be the jukebox hogger, the woman
standing from her seat, unafraid to request
another song, to solo that one about love,
or the one she couldn't help but relate
to the monotony of a stay-at-home mom;
a plight disguised by the melody inside her head,
as she'd mumble a few lyrics in Spanish,
childhood tunes of a happier Mexico,
then spin in circles the way my father

used to spin with her, lock their hips together,
and blur across the living room's
torn linoleum floor.

But standing in the doorway, perhaps picturing
a hypothetical of himself, the potential scenarios
of his own habits infused with impulse,
my father would simply step outside, pace
the porch and like a man down to his last pack
of cigarettes, inhale the night's firefly-filled air,
while I, seated across my mother, would watch
the bottles' condensation bleed onto my scattered
papers, the stack of homework she'd help me with,
the written and rewritten sentences discolored
by the growing rivulets, until they no longer resembled
English, but a language of wet graphite, a dialect
of wrinkled curves her own voice began to mirror,
as she'd lean over, belch a strawberry-sweet burp
above us, and pause as if about to apologize
for the embarrassment she thought I felt, unaware
I had already placed her somewhere else: a larger,
ageless room where the bartender would joke
about last calls, and where she'd chug another round
of on-the-house laughter, a gulp of relief
only her smile could distill.

LA PULGA

Sunday morning strolls along the frontage road
like a censer-swinging priest, scrapes its sunlight
against the corroded chain-link fence, between
the lines of traffic overflowing from the entrance,
where I already taste the scent of wet cilantro,
grilled onions, mixed meat, and eggs sizzled in a haze
of dust-shuffled heat; in a blanket of black exhaust
crawling across the pot-hole-riddled parking lot,
and through the rows of sunburned cars nudging
each other like buzzards on a corpse they've yet
to eat. I endure my grandfather's crooked parking,
the constant honking, the backseat acoustics of thin
music sprinkled in the air, those far-off plastic
speakers blaring songs with unpredictable trumpets,
and Spanish *gritos* slapped against my English-only ears.
Even if that language isn't mine, I attempt to translate
how I'm witnessed through every detail in this scene:
the light-skinned boy walking hand-in-hand with
his mud-brown grandparents, weaving through labyrinths
of $2 sock bundles, cases of tomatoes, strawberries,
knock-off DVDs, and mountains of used car parts ripe
with rust and unreliability, where my grandfather stops,
scans the price-tags for discounts, then moves us along
before the vendors stare long enough to make me believe
I've been kidnapped from the suburbs, that my grandparents
are here to parade their new prize around. And yet,
as we carve our presence farther in, as I imagine
my grandparents on the other end, watching as I leave,
I begin to feel I'm the one who's kidnapped them,
softly tugging their clay bodies through a market
they'll never see again; a weekend life remembered

only by the netted sacks of garlic bought, piled
like wreaths across the backseat where I lay
my head to rest; tired, thirsty, and ready to lead
these strangers to a better home.

GOATS

Of course I had to believe there was purpose to everything, the five a.m. chicken-feed routine, the cleaning of the shit-caked cages, the careful cow-milking, and the caring of runt pigs thirsty for their mother's teats; and there were the goats I thought of more as ponies when I released them to the hills, my favorite scene for the least favorite part of my day. Imagine a childhood of goats, each one vocal in their own goatish way, and imagine learning the word 'castration,' how sharp it sounded, how my father taught me how to hoist them by their legs, wide and firm, but calm enough not to resemble violence; we were cutting off their 'jewels' after all, our hands needed to be silent. The first few times I expected a joke, something about how *baaad* it must feel, and when I tried to crack one of my own, he shook his head, said he was glad they were too young to feel, that they wouldn't remember a thing. But I remember how he clamped the tissue with the elastrator, adjusted the rubber band while the buckling cried the way bucklings cried when they were out in the pasture, bending their soft backs beneath the barbed-wire fence, aware of what was coming when I caught up to them, grazed my fingers through their ears and nape, then carried their soft bodies back to the wooden table, where I gripped their hooves, flipped them upside down, and from where I watched—throughout the struggle—the moon on the drought-riddled plains, swollen, throbbing, and ready to fall.

BUZZARDS

Stoic, even as they strip a stray dog's carcass,
even as they autopsy its stomach, untangle
the knot of intestines, and redefine the mange
that once defined its skin, a wake of buzzards
feed by the splinters of our backyard fence,
beat their serrated wings and tails, hop
from one limb to the next, pushing for their share;
each as eager to burrow through maggots and meat
as the landscape is to turn them into symbols
for the biblical drought singed into the fields,
for the acres of expired crops, for the way the heat
stifles the afternoon with stasis and hallucination,
a belief that this could be purgatory,
and that whatever God one chooses has leased
this stretch of land to pay for our ancestors' sins,
spiting every generation for still calling it home.

And yet, there I am, listening to the heresy
of wind, to how steady my breathing becomes
as verse upon verse of sweat nooses my neck,
as my demeanor matches the buzzards', renders me
mute as I walk over, watch how they stop in mid-pluck,
and how, like my parents at the kitchen table,
they cock their bald and blood-wrinkled heads
at an angle that demands I say something important,
that waits for me to come closer, join them before
they take flight and forget the scraps they left behind,
those fresh and half-swallowed morsels
their shadows regurgitated for mine.

ROADSIDE

Mexico rises into view like a textbook description of a dead civilization;
its silhouette piercing the scaled soil, the streaks of afternoon mirages,

the caliche billowing across the windshield as my mother pulls into
    a roadside
stand. Still a few miles away, and I already see how poverty mimics

the effects of age, how it wears the fragmented skyline with corrosion,
subtracts layers of durability off a building's frame; how the city mirrors

the black-and-white photos of abandoned warzones; how a fence
    can lose
its purpose, become symbolic, while the river below it bleeds a history

of unsuccessful bodies no one ever claims. Before we cross over, graze
the peripheries of those who haven't tried their hand at an exodus—

the barefooted boys selling Chiclets, the old and toothless women
seated
on the bridge, the sleeping infants strapped in serapes to their mothers'
    chests—

we weave, like we do every weekend, through rows of shoulder-high
    water fountains,
pattern-painted pots, and ceramic statues of Aztec gods ready
    for someone's yard,

each a variation of mud-brown and red, and as hot as stove-grates when
    I run
my fingertips along their rims, note the way my mother does the same.

She doesn't pull back though, doesn't squeal or flinch, her endurance

for pain
callused on her hands like the callused face of the old woman on
    a lawn chair

beneath a tarp, where they begin to make small-talk in their muffled
Mexican tongues. Behind them sits the woman's Chevy, whitewashed

and windowless, its bed stacked with the inventory she didn't take down,
and I recall those playground jokes about how in spite of the small space

they have, Mexicans can fit anything inside a car; a punchline that whether
    I find
funny or not, I imagine she'll embody when she towers her ceramics
    back inside

her truck, aware that even as my mother scans the worn-out pricetags
of each pot, we aren't going to buy a thing. And as they exchange
    a few nods

like outdated currency, I watch the old woman's hand reach out and touch
our shadows the way old women touch everything that isn't theirs, feeling

the indifference with which we slip between her grip, how the sunlight
    cracks
our skin like pottery as it breaks.

TUMBLEWEEDS

They came around like lost dogs looking for a place to rest, prickly, small, tangled on the splintered planks of oak; a midsummer migration spit from the horizon's bleeding mouth, where they wandered up the steps of our front porch. There was no movie-bounce or wind, no cowboy, crickets, no symbolism not already known, their wobbly march scraping the mounds of blistered dirt, because our yard was just as dry as them, shriveled stiffly like our skin. Football fields away, they'd rise and cluster, forged by the heat in just the right frame, that I'd think of them as the devil's knuckles, still digging through the limbo he'd been buried in, while I sat buried in this blaze, collecting all the tumbleweeds in my head, stacking them until I built the family of snowmen again, parched replicas of my father, mother, and me in the center of this scene, like mannequins out of some Manhattan project; our faces smiling at the melting sun, waiting for the mushroom cloud to blow our way.

ENCORE

Mid-March. Mid-stride, and as I walk once more
through the middle of some childhood fair, watching

the scenery unfold in medias res, the sun begins to refuse
its role again, letting nightfall and the faint genesis of wind

calcify our sweat, dilute the prize-winning, cattle-scented shit
caked throughout the show grounds, which the crowd I join,

ignoring my presence as much as I try to ignore theirs,
doesn't notice, or doesn't care about, too enthralled

with the turkey legs, the sausage sticks, the funnel cakes,
and the red roll of tickets they pull from their pockets, presenting

the stubs like tithes at the entrance. Together, we take our seats,
applaud, shout, vocalize whatever slur of impulsive words

spill from our mouths, and as the scene takes on a hint
of the religious—a need to let the tongue speak what the body

cannot—I find myself gnawing on the deep-fried ambiance,
on the aisles of bleacher laughter galloping like the bareback

broncos below, where the rodeo counts its final seconds down,
and the mud-splattered clowns corral the rider away

from his shaken disappointment. Tonight we gauge happiness
by how hard a body hits the ground, or by the amount of car metal

crushed when one by one the monster trucks come out, rev a lap
around, and, as if echoing the ancient bloodlust of coliseums,

initiate their first strikes, bulldozing through junkyard-rusted rows
of Toyotas, Hondas, Nissans and Volkswagen vans, shattering

their small and foreign-made engines like glass, because even if
this show plays out on the southern tip of Texas, and the landscape

is nothing more than fallow farmland, the attitude is still American.
And after Bigfoot, Snakebite and Gravedigger invent their own rules

for gravity, suspend all 12,000 pounds from one dirt ramp to another,
the lights dim across the stands, and out rolls the encore,

the forty-foot Robosaurus spitting fire from its metal teeth
and nostrils, transforming from a semi-trailer into what I imagine

plagues an automaker's nightmares; clawing through doors
and rooftops, lifting everything that's already crushed,

and splitting it in half before roasting the ribs of fiberglass
from the inside out, all while the scent of diesel, sprinkled throughout

the stadium, induces in us a sense that breaking something,
anything, is the quickest way to make it ours.

ACKNOWLEDGEMENTS

Many thanks to the editors of the following magazines and journals in which some of these poems first appeared:

American Literary Review: "Cactus"
basalt: "Christmas" and "Toothless"
Bluestem: "Seasonal"
Chicago Quarterly Review: "Tamales"
The Country Dog Review: "Skin"
Euphony: "Clothesline" and "Intermission"
The Florida Review: "Roadside"
Ghost Town: "Telenovela"
Hayden's Ferry Review: "White Gold"
Huizache: "Fowl" and "Fence"
The Los Angeles Review: "Dogs"
The McNeese Review: "Piñata"
Nashville Review: "Lemonade," "Locks," and "Last Call"
New England Review: "La pulga"
Quiddity: "Lips" and "Meat"
Steel Toe Review: "Ax," "Cats," and "Heifer"
storySouth: "Tumbleweeds"
Squalorly: "Goats" and "Lucha libre"
Sugar House Review: "Salt"
Water~Stone Review: "Ventriloquist"
Weber-The Contemporary West: "Exodus" and "Trash"
Yemassee: "Buzzards"
"La pula" and "Roadside" were featured in *Poetry Daily*.

I am grateful to my mentors and friends who helped shape many of the poems in this book: Steven Schneider, Emmy Pérez, Daniel Mendoza, and Charles McGregor. Thank you to Meg Reid, Kate McMullen, and Betsy Teter for their kindness and support. A special thank you to my wife Norma for her love and encouragement, as well as to Patrick Whitfill for his keen eye and belief in my work. Finally, thank you to my mother, father, and sister— you will always be my inspiration.

HUB CITY
PRESS

HUB CITY PRESS is the South's premier independent literary press. Focused on finding and spotlighting new and extraordinary voices from the American South, the press has published over ninety high-caliber literary works. Hub City is interested in books with a strong sense of place and is committed to introducing a diverse roster of lesser-heard Southern voices. We are funded by the National Endowment for the Arts, the South Carolina Arts Commission, and hundreds of donors across South Carolina.

RECENT HUB CITY PRESS POETRY

Rodeo in Reverse • Lindsey Alexander

Magic City Gospel • Ashley M. Jones

Wedding Pulls • J.K. Daniels

Punch • Ray McManus

Pantry • Lilah Hegnauer

Voodoo For the Other Woman • Angela Kelly

Waking • Ron Rash

Garamond MT Pro
10.9/14